Environmental Refugees- Causes and Economic Effects.

Minhajul Abedin

ISBN 978-93-5458-926-3

Published in India 2021 by Pencil

A brand of
One Point Six Technologies Pvt. Ltd.
123, Building J2, Shram Seva Premises,
Wadala Truck Terminal, Wadala (E)
Mumbai 400037, Maharashtra, INDIA
E connect@thepencilapp.com
W www.thepencilapp.com

Author biography

Minhajul Abedin (1996-Present) .I'm an Indian Environmentalist, I was born in the Indian state of Assam. I have completed my graduation in Environmental Science from Amity University Kolkata. I have written a book chapter for the famous book " Industrial Technologies for Bioethanol Production from Lignocellulosic Biomass" which was published by Taylor and Francis Group.

Book chapter link- https://www.taylorfrancis.com/chapters/edit/10.1201/9780429265099-4/industrial-technologies-bioethanol-

CONTENTS

Environmental Refugees and Its Types

Environmental refugees are the people who are forced to leave their habitat temporarily or permanently due to the sudden change in their local environment. The changes may be caused naturally or triggered by humans.

Types of Environmental Refugees:

1. Climate Refugee.
2. Political Refugee.

Climate Refugee:

A climate refugee can be defined as a person who has been forced to leave his or her own habitat due to the negative effects of climate change on their environment.

Political Refugee:

A political Refugee is any individual who is unable to stay in his/her own country because of civil war, citizenship dispute, and political persecution. Political refugees also include asylum seekers. These factors force people to migrate internally or across the border.

Latest Refugee Crisis

Venezuela is going through political turmoil since 1999. But after the death of President Hugo Chavez, the political situation deteriorate. The increase in unemployment and market inflation has forced millions to flee their country seeking food, work and better life.

Millions of Venezuelans have left their country as of mid-2021, including 186,800 refugees, 952,300 asylum-seekers, and 3.9 million Venezuelans displaced abroad.

Countries Driving Global Refugee Crisis

Serial No	Country
1	Syria
2	Afghanistan
3	Somalia
4	Sudan
5	Democratic Republic of Congo
6	The central African Republic
7	Myanmar
8	Venezuela
9	Mexico
10	Colombia

How to Solve Political Refugee Crisis

1. Figure out the root cause and solve it.
2. The United Nation should pay special attention towards the countries whose political condition is hostile.
3. Resettlement of the refugees. It is a vital solution for most vulnerable refugees.
4. The Global leaders and International agencies need to put saving life first . They must participate in rescue operations.
5. Stop racism and trafficking .The United Nation Peace Keeping Force should be deployed in the refugee affected areas to stop trafficking and exploitation of refugees.
6. The Global leaders should take initiatives to solve the political issues of the countries those are facing leadership crisis. e.g. Myanmar, South Sudan , Afghanistan etc.
7. International ban should be imposed on the countries those are violating human rights.

8. There must be special law for the weapon selling countries.I.e they can not sell weapon to the country who is violating human rights.

9. The UN should urge states not to return refugees to their country until the problems are solved.

*** None of the above mentioned solutions are impossible to achieve , if politicians and international agencies make commitment to solve it

Climate Refugees.

Climate refugees are the people who are forced to leave their habitat due to long-term or sudden changes in their local environment.

Factors causing the climate refugees

- Droughts
- Desertification
- Sea-level Rise
- The climate refugees also include the refugees caused due to environmental phenomena (Tsunami, Flooding, Cyclones, etc.).

The above factors force internal migration or migration across the borders.

- According to UNHCR, there are about 40.1 Million climatic refugees in the world.
- The number of climatic refugees is more than political refugees.

Climate Change and Climate Refugee

The Earth is going through a broad set of global change, scarcity of resources, biodiversity loss, rapid industrialization and urbanization.

Climate change is one of the most concerned phenomenon as it is one of the driver of the global environmental change. Over the previous six-seven decades climate change received strong focus from the scientists , law makers , global leaders and United Nations . At present it is considered as the most dangerous global threat that not only includes environmental problems but also effects the socioeconomic structures and the over all development process.The Climate change has introduced a new social communities called "Climatic Refugees".

The United Nations High Commissioner for Refugees states that more refugees are displaced by environmental catastrophes. At, present there are 40.1 million climatic refugees and by 2050 it would reach up to 300 Millions. The cumulative effects of climate change exacerbate food , water, health insecurity, loss of biodiversity, loss of different types of ecosystems, environmental degradation and human insecurity through war, political conflict and violence in the different regions of the world.

Hence, the socioeconomic structure are undermined in those regions (Countries) where the affected people are compelled to switch over occupations for livelihood . These are the people who no longer can ensure a secure livelihood in their countries. The refugees have induced a notable change in the whole economic structure of the host countries.

Countries Facing Different Environmental Change

The most common disasters are flood and cyclone, recent IPCC (Intergovernmental Panel on Climate Change) assessment report reveals that over the last two decades cyclone and flood have became more frequent and devastating for many countries. A new legal frame work is needed to address the different challenges faced by communities (Climatic Refugees) severely affected by climate change.

- low-lying countries may become wholly uninhabitable if the sea levels continue to rise.

- Larger countries such as India and China with significant coastal populations may be able to accommodate internal migration from the area affected by sea-level rise, but need significant assistance in doing so.

- A rapid number of natural disasters such as tsunami, typhoons, and floods is forcing people to take shelter elsewhere in the country or across the border.

Drought	Flood	Severe Cyclone	Sea Level Rise
Malawi	Bangladesh	Philippines	Senegal
Niger	China	Sri Lanka	Zimbabwe
Sudan	India	India	Maldives
Chad	Cambodia	China	Bangladesh
Iran	Thailand	Madagascar	Vietnam
Kenya	Mozambique	USA	Indonesia

Image: Flood Barrier

Drought ,Desertification & Environmental Refugees

Drought and desertification are two of the many factors driving the global refugee crisis. United Nations Convention to Combat Desertification (U.N.C.C.D) estimates that about 135 million people may be displaced by 2045 as a result of desertification.

Drought may be caused due to the following reasons:

- Rainfall or precipitation deficiency.
- Deforestation.
- Drying out surface water.
- Global warming.
- Overgrazing.
- Deforestation.
- Overuse of water resources is one of the leading factors responsible for desertification.

* Every year about 10-12 million hectares of productive lands become barren due to drought and desertification.

* The Gobi Desert (China) is expanding very rapidly. The desert expands 10000 sq. km every year threatening fertile land and the livelihood of the local people.

Image: Drought

*** Office of the Coordination of Humanitarian Affairs (OCHA) estimated that 10 million people across the Horn of Africa(Djibouti, Eritrea, Somalia, etc) are facing a severe food crisis following a prolonged drought in the region, experiencing the worst drought in 70 years**

Effects of Drought

- Drying out water resources.
- Reduction of soil quality.
- Migration of people,
- Reduced Crop Yields.
- Hunger, malnutrition, and deaths.

Prevention of Drought and Desertification

1. Planting drought-resistant plants.
2. Sustainable use of groundwater.
3. Integrating the use of land for farming and grazing where conditions are favorable.
4. Protecting the vegetation cover.
5. Plantation of local plants that use less water.
6. Integrated farming system.
7. Smarter irrigation system.
8. Rainwater harvesting.

Image: Drought Affected Area Across the World

Relation Between Environmental Scarcities and Refugees

The scarcity of natural resources is one of the major factor for the migration of people.Environmental scarcity is also responsible for the outbreak of many conflicts.

Environmental scarcity can lead to civil unrest by the following ways:

- Resource Capture.→ when a resource become limited, it often becomes more valuable. The increase in the value of the resource may motivate powerful countries or groups to take control of the resource, which may lead to violent activity like war

- Ecological Marginalization→ when vital resources such as water,land and forest etc becomes limited due to population unequal access and population explosion ,the people tend to move into an ecologically sensitive areas such as hillsides and forests this leads to the further degradation of resources.

Water Scarcity and Environmental Refugees

The scarcity of water can force people to migrate in search of new habitats. Water is both a push and pulls factor for migration since agriculture is the primary employment in most developing countries.

Cause of Water Scarcity

- Water Pollution.→ pollution of freshwater sources like rivers and lakes by the industries through waste discharge.

- *Drought.→ a drought is a condition of an area when it lacks average rainfall. The prolonged drought can dry up surface water which may lead to overuse of groundwater, as a result, water scarcity may occur.

- Agriculture→ Majority of the available freshwater is used for agricultural purposes. It is estimated that 60% of the water used in agriculture gets wasted due to insufficient agricultural methods.

- Population Explosion→ As the human population is increasing very rapidly, there is a demand for freshwater, which may result in additional pressure on freshwater sources.

- The Global Water Institute estimated that around a 700-800nmillion people in 43 countries suffer from water scarcity.

- Data on access to water suggests that the largest number of people without access to water live in North Africa, the Middle East, Sub Sahara, and Central Asia, etc.

Mediterreanean Sea
LEBANON
SYRIA
Sea of Galilee
ISRAEL
West Bank
Negev Desert
JORDAN
IRAQ
IRAN
EGYPT
KUWAIT
Persian Gulf
SAUDI ARABIA
BAHRAIN
QATAR
Gulf of Oman
UNITED ARAB EMIRATES
OMAN
Red Sea
Sanaa
YEMEN
IN LESS THAN 10 YEARS
half the world's population will be living in water-stressed areas.

Global Water Conflicts

The term water conflicts means the conflicts between groups, states and countries over an access to water resources. Water conflicts appear through out the history.

Reasons for Conflicts

- Territorial Disputes
- Fight for Resources.
- Strategic Advantage

Notable Water Conflicts

- Conflict between Turkey, Syria and Iraq for the water sharing of Euphrates riveer.
- Nile River Conflict between Egypt , Ethiopia and Sudan.

- Conflict between India and China on hydro electric Dam constructed Brahmaputra river.
- Bolivian Water war , it as a series of protests took place all over Bolivia in the year 1999-2000 against rice of drinking water prices.During the protest 6 were killed and 175 people were injured.

Solutions to Water Scarcity.

- Re use of water and Effective Treatment Technology.
- Desalination of Sea Water.
- Proper water Management.
- Water Conservation.
- Repairing of Infrastructure and Maintenance.

Refugee Host Countries

The refugee crisis affects specific countries and regions disproportionately.

There are 19.9 million refugees under United Nations High Commission For Refugees (UNHCR) mandate, out of these 85% of the refugee are hosted by developing countries.

Top 10 Refugee Hosting Countries.

Countries	No of refugees (In Millions)
Turkey	3.7
Jordan	2.9
Colombia	1.7
Lebanon	1.5
Pakistan	1.4

Uganda	1.3
Germany	1.2
Sudan	1.0
Iran	0.9
Bangladesh	0.7

Economic Impact of Refugees

Environmental refugees have a very huge impact on the economy, the number of refugees displaced every year is on rising. The World Food Programme provides food aid in cash or in-kind to these refugees. The economic impact on host countries is complicated and little understood. The United Nations and other international organizations are spending billions of dollars on refugees.

The UNHCR is the organization mainly responsible for monitoring refugee conditions and helping them by providing food aid, health assistance and constructing refugee camps, etc. The UNHCR is funded by different developed countries. Some countries like Kuwait, Norway, USA and Canada, etc, give millions of dollars from their national treasury to UNHCR.

UNHCR Donors List 2017

Countries/ Organization	Amount in Millions
USA	1400

European Union	470
Germany	336
Japan	175
United Kingdom	103
Sweden	121
Kuwait	120
Netherlands	78
Spain	68
Australia	53
Qatar	26
Belgium	19
Saudi Arabia	17
UAE	9

Negative Impact of Refugees on host Countries

Refugees compete with the local populations for resources like water , land (for housing), food and Medical services. The long term presence of refugees leads to more demand of ….

- Education
- Natural Resources
- Energy Demand
- Transportation
- Employment
- Health Facilities
- Social Services etc.

The above factor may cause inflationary pressures on price and depress wages.

- Large refugee population in a country creates a strain on local administration, the host countries spend millions of rupees for keeping the refugees alive and ensuring their security.

- The large scale presence of refugees invariably constitutes a heavy burden for the host countries particularly Less Developing Countries(LDC).

- Human waste disposal can contaminate local surface and ground water and cause the spread of diseases

Conclusion

The Current refugee crisis is a catastrophe affecting millions of families, endangering the stability of the host countries, there is a little chance to return some of the refugees to their home nation because of the hostile situation.Managing the crisis and mitigating its worst crisis needs

courage , strong leadership and political will .All the countries must have responsibility for predicting, planning and managing the impact of the environmental change The civil society, national government and the international organizations need to determine weather the appropriate organization/institution :

- Taking care of the citizens displaced by the environmental cause.
- Are using holistic and human right based approaches to the refugees.
- Are doing enough to preserve and protect the environment.

- Are prepared to face and respond any kind of natural disasters.

The heavy price that the host countries have to pay is widely recognized , the best way to mitigate this problem is the international authorities must focus on the refugee situations and they must take strong action against human right violation and political prosecution and there must be additional support to the host countries.

UNHCR Refugee DATA

According to the United Nations High Commissioner for Refugees.

- There are 35.9 Million political refugees (As of 11 Nov 2021)

Image: Syrian Children at Za"atari Refugee Camp, Jordan

1. 19.9 Million under UNHCR mandate

2. 5.4 Million Palestinian refugees.
3. 4.4 Million asylum seekers.
4. 5.1 Million Venezuelan Refugees
5. More than 1.1 Million Rohingya Refugees.

According to **UNHCR**latest data

There are **84 MILLION**

Forcibly displaced people worldwide

An estimated 35.28 million (42%) of the 84 million forcibly displaced people are children below 18 years of age.

Abstract

The book reviews the existing research papers and also informs about the **environmental scarcities**, **environmental refugees**, and the impact of refugees on the economy. The book also highlights the types of environmental refugees, the root cause of refugees. It discusses the **natural disasters**, scarcity of resources, and their relation with environmental refugees.

This book focuses on the Policies developed by international agencies like **UNEP**, **UNHCR**, and **World Bank**, etc. To combat environmental degradation. It is being said that the impact of environmental change in refugees is critical and special attention must be paid to policies and research to figure out the interaction between environmental change and wider economic, political, and social factors.

Introduction

The scarcities of natural resources has been enhanced due to Climate Change, natural disasters as well .It has threatened the livelihood of millions of people around the world. In, recent years the concept of environmental refugees has gained new importance. The term environmental refugee was coined by EL-Hinnawi , describes people who have been forced to leave their traditional habitat , temporarily or permanently , because of a marked environmental disruption (Natural/ Triggered by human) that seriously affect the life of the people.

The Environmental refugees tend to come from developing countries.

According to the Centre of Disease Control and Prevention , since the early 1950s most emergencies involving refugees have taken place in the less developing countries where resource are inadequate to support the population. The number of displaced people are rising worldwide .Of, these the number of forced migration is increasing rapidly, because of economic and environmental conditions is growing more rapidly than refugees from political strife. The refugees not only imposes a negative impact on the economy of the “host countries” but also the global economy.

www.ingramcontent.com/pod-product-compliance
Lightning Source LLC
LaVergne TN
LVHW050427160726
843469LV00041B/1269

* 9 7 8 9 3 5 4 5 8 9 2 6 3 *